Who

Who

Release the Who

KEARA COMBS

J. Kenkade
PUBLISHING®

LITTLE ROCK, ARKANSAS

Who
Copyright © 2021 by Keara Combs

J. Kenkade Publishing
6104 Forbing Rd
Little Rock, AR 72209
www.jkenkadepublishing.com
Facebook.com/jkenkadepublishing

J. Kenkade Publishing is a registered trademark.

Printed in the United States of America

ISBN 978-1-955186-22-3

J. Kenkade Publishing is not the editor or proofreader of this book. ⊠he proofreading option was not selected by Author.

⊠his book recounts actual events in the life of Keara Combs according to the author's recollection and per-spective. Some of the identifying details may have been changed to respect the privacy of those involved.

⊠he views expressed in this book are those of the author and do not necessarily reflect the views of Publisher.

Table of Contents

Dedication

For everyone out there spiritual or non spiritual. Dedicated to invite everyone into a spirit world. Specifically for everyone out there for history matters. Normally I wouldn't dedicate things to anyone but here's one for the world. What we normally wouldn't want to write or mostly talk about. The healings of our minds and what we've been through in our lives. This is what makes us who we are and who we are afraid to become. This book demonstrates what we hold on to and should let go of. Taking full action over the things we will not do what scares us from it. It's dedicated to hope that somebody understands how the mind works and how to deal with our own sufferings releases you mentally and physically.

Acknowledgments

For everyone out there spiritual or non spiritual. Dedicated to invite everyone into a spirit world. Specifically for everyone out there for history matters. Normally I wouldn't dedicate things to anyone but here's one for the world. What we normally wouldn't want to write or mostly talk about. The healings of our minds and what we've been through in our lives. This is what makes us who we are and who we are afraid to become. This book demonstrates what we hold on to and should let go of. Taking full action over the things we will not do what scares us from it. It's dedicated to hope that somebody understands how the mind works and how to deal with our own sufferings releases you mentally and physically.

CHAPTER 1

❧

Home

Wanting to kill myself or run away always took place in my mind during depression. Growing up here with family I still ended up developing a stable mind set after all . Finding myself was the best things starting out and finishing. Which would sound weird to say because it wasn't easy. It was the best thing that ever happened to me to be around family most of the time because what was changing during the times. Lying in the bed at night crying myself to sleep.

During these times there was many things happening and going on around me. Meeting new people having fun enjoying life. Pretty much didn't care about the ride just was living. Occasionally most things I did was based upon my mind set. Horribly I found myself going to Pulaski County Dentition Center for a jungle juice once.

Figures that kicking it was the easy part I eventually got over in life for a while. According to what has been happening in my life I was messing out on what could change in my life. Especially when you don't care how your living and doing things in your life. Based upon the choices I've made I've learned to self discipline myself. From the things people and places which were taking me off track.

Corruption isn't what just happens to people it's in people and they create it. So what do you do when you want to change but you feel like you can't. Mentally I feel that everyone can change no matter who your around or what your fight is. Sometimes if you lack strength you go through things that will strengthen you. Real strength is how far you are willing to go no matter what. What do you say about your actions that would allow you to change.

Did I think I would ever make it from my mental stage by myself. People never will understand why someone is naturally depressed.

Mentally only that person knows. Being in a mental stage doesn't mean your mental it means your suffering in a area that causes different reactions. What reaction my stages have caused me. Mixed emotions behavioral actions from sufferings and lack.

So what causes us to keep pushing our sufferings away. Really I hid all my sufferings. Naturally our actions so that we are suffering. To some things we do we think they're right. Suffering had me and bad and good places.

What do some of us deal with that we rather not share. Truthfully why do we still hold on to what hurts if your suppose to be happy. How do you make suffering yourself a easy way to deal with your sufferings. Let's start with Abuse, neglect, mistreatment, being raped or losing someone you love. Do you define yourself by what people have done to you and what your going through.

Being so hurt and along makes people depressed. You have to endure the pain you have to learn about the pain you have to figure out why. I was frighten to be suffering I didn't know how deep I was going to be in that place. No one had control over the way I felt or they couldn't change it. The feelings just mentally had me really lost.

Every time I would look up I was enduring something. How am I going to get out of this. Why do people help you have never talked to. How did I know I was enduring something alone if many people was around. All the answers I was looking for them but god found me and answered me every time.

Why was I mostly hurt being at home what was happening to me there. Was it the people I loved hurting me or the people I thought I trusted. Did they mean it and did I get over it. Certain situations I was going through I didn't know what to do but I knew I had god. I knew I was going to end up being hurt by people mostly because I had a destination to reach.

I figured out how to deal with my depression I tell god about my problems which he already knew about. Afterwards I would deal with what I was going through and do things that would make me feel better. Going and talking with people about my problems and the things I would through. Never looked for people to fix them but I choose to not run from them eventually but face them. So why was I wanting to kill myself if I didn't run from my problems.

What does it mean to not let yourself get so low but you become low. Some times people have a huge affect on you. You become tired of being hurt and that's being in a depressed stage. Mostly people was always around. So why all the people around but nobody there when you need them the most.

Battling with things by yourself or even with people can be tuff. Broken chains is the things we face but over come. How many times were you suffering with some thing in you over came it. Does it still hurt how come we don't face that fact that people don't control our minds. So we actually are able to over come things and get over them.

I started using a notebook to write down my problems. Then I went to people and found other things I could enjoy doing. Eventually I found no reason to stay hurt if I found other people to encourage a difference for me. The healing starts with control of your mind and sometimes to find peace and happiness within yourself. Mostly you need god in your life we miss the reason we still live.

Lately I've been feeling like I shouldn't be around people as often as I should. I once was in a stage were I felt depressed all the time. Never understood why this feeling puts you inside a deep tunnel vision. So depressed I had no control what's so ever over my mind. Being so suicidal and lost is the worst stage someone could be in.

CHAPTER 2

※

Demons

Seeing demons in my dreams use to scare me. Did I wonder why I always would see them. Were they after me and what did they want. Understanding that they are the dead taking over people. It would sound crazy to say I was scared of things I would see in a dream.

These dreams start happening everyday. I started seeing them physically sometimes. It was so scary at first but that's before I got use to seeing them. Praying was always my first instincts to finding out why I kept seeing them. After dramatically understanding the reason I would see them. Why do people think you have a mental issue when you see and understand things they don't.

Believing that we all might actually have something we rather not learn about. People called me weird mental or quiet all the time. I use to hardly keep myself from around people so much. Sometimes people are distant because their trying to understand something about themselves or going through something. So why don't people ask instead of make fun of it.

Once I became un afraid of understanding what I kept seeing I started searching for who was showing me it more. Sometimes I use to think I was losing my mind because what I was able to see. Instead I knew that moment what a true demon was. So I knew eventually I would have a lot of problems happening in my life and with people by what I could see. Not because of me but because of what many people didn't like about me.

It was a spiritual thing. Did that ever mean people were suppose to like it. I've never been a people person until I got around some outgoing people. What do demons do and what do they take. Making someone's life horrible or trying to take good things from God away.

Mostly they can't anything god has given away.

Does this mean be afraid of people no and what they might worship. Everyone goes through something regardless of a spiritual situation or who you worship. So what was all the darkness in my life. What changes are you trying to accomplish in life. Do you feel like your in a fight.

Wonder why no one likes you when your different and you just want to share it with everyone. Some people may think you want to be better than them but your just different. People don't have to understand that. I've never been ashamed of myself I only Wondered why people wasn't interested in what I was telling them.

Why does it hurt to not understand something. Maybe it's the lack of knowledge or wisdom. We seek after the wrong things in life. So we're looking for understanding. Why shouldn't it start with ourselves. So spiritually we all get attacked good or bad.

Eventually do people want to be happy. Why do they risk their own lives for the sake of really not being happy. If we're happy why do we want to hurt others. Have it been important to seek your own self. To understand what it is you need and want that you don't want to use other people for. Spiritually understanding that people have no spiritual right to tell you what to believe.

These things grow on the inside of us. Is death worth everything on earth. What have caused me to suffer from this spiritual category. Learning what I didn't understand finding out and looking up to who knew. It caused people to turn against me and I could do nothing but tell somebody anyhow.

What was I struggling with who understood. When you see something do you talk about it. How do people make you feel. We should understand it doesn't matter how people feel about what goes on in our mind. Talking about it will help them to eventually understand.

People can't understand what they don't have control over. But what if theirs people who don't care or I have no one to talk to. Of course you do I've learned to look up. People hardly listened to me I think people I would talk to wasn't interested. Did that stop me from sharing I believed that it needed to be heard so I kept telling it over and over

Sooner or later I got tired so I focused on what I seen for myself. It was hard enough for me to deal with people and suffering from what had end up keep seeing. It was a nightmare but turned out to be just right for me to see. Mostly I would come under attack more often. From car wrecks to panic attacks to depression to bad thoughts to juvenile to pinnacle point to bad people bad things happening over and over.

How did I deal with this and these things that kept happening. I found nothing wrong with them until I realized it wasn't what I was doing it was who I was. To keep putting myself in situations that I would clearly see the trouble it would get me into. I ended leading myself in directions of different things and people. Couldn't expect them to be perfect but I did expect myself to become better.

What's it like being on a tuff road trying to be better but can't find better. It was in myself I had to stop what I was doing in order to focus on the change. Being interested in different things might cause you to hurt and loose people. It sure does help in the long run to be different also wanting to be better. Did I then realize what I really was surrounded by and what made it difficult.

So did I ever stop seeing what I was seeing even if people wasn't listening. Even if it was badly hurting me if I was going through all that. Did I still change was I able to do better. Did I want to judge people because I knew something else. I stayed true to myself and what I understood about myself the change was because of what I was seeing.

Enjoying the fact that we don't physical see them but they are in some of us. But how do you know that how do people know what's in someone else. They don't but they see it. Did I ever stop being myself or going around me does this mean I am not normal. Everyone has something they deal with that doesn't mean they don't have life outside of that.

Every night I cried out and fought everyday spiritually and emotionally . I never knew how long I would be in these fights. Some of the things I would deal with would feel like too much that I could bare but I've always gotten the hang of it.   Being so Spiritual I knew god had allowed some things in my life to   happen for me to be able to overcome. Most the time in these cases I would always fight back.

Who

What really happens when we don't actually know where to turn. When we feel attacked all the time or as I'd there's demons after us. I use the only solution which is god I have became witnessed to believe that god is the biggest protector above all my situations and circumstances. Once I became spiritually aware of my own battles and fights I knew that I would be able to fight them . Did I know the demons I was fighting did I understand why they kept coming.

Before I got saved I didn't know why there were fights and battles. I couldn't understand the spiritual awakenings nor the strong holds. Do people believe in spiritual warfare . I used to be very afraid of the things I was up against. Sometimes I would have to get to fact of knowing if it would actually scare me or not.

My first attack was in my dream. I started having attacks in my dream then physically and mental attacks. No matter what I always knew some how to get through it. So I always had a fight it never failed. The strangest thing about seeing demons is actually seeing them.

CHAPTER 3

❧

Church

Growing up in church I didn't like it. I started off singing in the choir then I did the usher board were I greeted people at the doors. Mostly I enjoyed that better it was kind of fun and a way to be up I could walk off anytime. Our parents or grandparents made us go every Sunday and maybe every Wednesday for bible study . One thing about the choir I didn't like was standing up in front of all those people singing but I got use to it after awhile.

I figured church was pretty important for us to need when we're young our parents and grandparents make us go. However now why don't we try as hard to go as we did then. Church seems different when your younger. Seems as if people just go to look cute. Truth is I've never physically got baptized at church. Before I started to go to church I never actually knew there was a god and Jesus . In fact I thought god and Jesus was the same person.

Is church only based upon preaching. Its actually based upon many things. A place of healing worship and the word of God. Getting baptized isn't just for people that are going through something. You could just simply believe that Jesus Christ died for you and you'll Be saved.

But I wonder what makes other people go to church. Is it the savings of your soul or do you just love god. What Interest us about going to church. Is it your pain and the things you've been through that allows you to enter into his house. The first time I cried in church was when they were singing one of my favorite singers from church was singing.

I would always watch people get the " holy ghost" and wonder what are they doing. I never understood but at least I was interested in knowing. I use to play church with some of my relatives at home and we would act as preachers and church members who would get the "holy ghost". We would take turns being a pastor. I knew I would be a Christian I've always honestly loved church.

During the times I did go to church I've never got up to do anything. I just sat there in stared. If I would get up it would be because I got use to being in there. The pastor and choir members would always wonder. The purpose of church Is worshipping god and obeying rather not if we're understanding. If people are not sure rather to go to church my answer would be you don't even have to believe or understand it.

Its totally there for you to believe and learn to believe so you would understand his word . Coming from someone who didn't know god or Jesus. Neither did I like church one bit. Which is weird because I always end up going and playing church roles anyhow. I participated in everything the church had I went to bible study Sunday class the after Sunday school church trips and church events.

Who says church can't be fun it's not just church. Once you start to go in just let it flow you'll flow with it. I've even had church boyfriends that's how much I didn't understand it. Sneaking around the church with my little friends being fast. Being young you don't understand stuff so we mostly think with our head not our brains. What does that mean we aren't prefect and we will mess up constantly.

Do you ever wonder why you have to tell all your problems to the pastor in front of everyone. I use to think it would be embarrassing or too many people being in your business. Eventually I realized that that's god house and this only means the fact that everyone is welcome and their situations. Everyone in there are family and it's nothing god can't handle. So if we decide to ever share our situations we know your inviting god into your life.

So how did I let go of my problems if I've never walked down. I pray and talk to god personally on a personal level. Everyone's situation will be different along with there experience. Not only when you get saved are you committing yourself to god. Your also committing yourself to his words and everything he says. It's not easy following god but it's love joy and happiness. The reasons it's hard for people to stay in church is because they can't seem to commit to the truth about this world. Church is a place of peace don't be afraid of what's healing and saves.

Why do I say that if I didn't stay in church. I actually did I found another church and it's my church home I've been going there for 4 years. I'm committed to god now more than ever. I've been through everything with god he has never left me neither abandon me. I trust what he says because he has never failed me. Why should you trust or how can you if you never been or don't know god.

People probably thought I was wasting my time going to church or even listening to my pastor. But they have saved me also. If wasn't for my pastor who God sent I wouldn't be were I am. It's not easy but because I have a ear to hear what he says I'm saved and guided along the way. How did I know that I felt that.

I believe church isn't just based upon religious belief or what god someone worships. Everything about just is based upon the true facts about what's happening in our world and the god of our heavens. Mostly I found myself the type of person to always want to go to church. I've never knew what true faith was until I found myself going to church gaining faith and learning about faith. True faith was based upon what someone had a belief in.

When I was younger I thought church was silly. I figured it was fake and not so important. Wondering why there's people singing in the choir. What was the point of us giving an offering nothing makes since when you don't care.

Every Sunday I went to church on the church van. I would be happy to get up and go. And once we go we would sit on the same bench. Directly in the front where the pastor is. The pastor would stare all the time. I thought it would be wired to sit so close up.

I didn't be seen to get up and do anything. Eventually once we would start going I would sneak and try to sit anywhere

CHAPTER 4

Battles

Things we go through now or previously were ridiculously horrible. What kind of fights have you had. I've had spiritual fights physical fights mental fights and more. So most of my battles started right when I was in middle school. Being saved you actually go through a lot and you have to deal with a lot it's not easy.

What kind of battles do saved people have the same as anybody else. We could go through as much more as someone else. Saved people deal mostly with things spiritual. So why did I constantly get in fights and things if I was saved it's part of believing. You could be on so many levels of death experiences but not actually dying. I've always prayed and god was right there protecting me. He makes sure it's not something you wouldn't be able to handle alone. The reason for that is because he will be right there to save you every time. Rather some one understand it or not god protects you even in your worst battles. The worst battle was dealing with the devil literally.

What has ran your life is it your battles. Is it ruining your life do you feel like your life is over. Maybe the things we go through suppose to make you stronger. Telling you rather to let go or stay strong. Who is the most people you were in battles with do they still come around.

Growing up I didn't know how to deal with many things. That wasn't always the case I had people I could go to for help all the time. Time after the time I use to ask myself what was it I was actually going through. Was it the same pains over and over again. Finding out through life you experience things and originally you'll just either have to face them or handle them.

Why does it feel like the pain never ends or what's this emptiness we feel. Is it were lonely or do we feel sadness that were alone. Throughout my growing life experiences I've realized how much I've went through just being twenty three years old. But I've loved and cherished my life and understand everything I've went through. At Soon as you get away from hurt why does it want to keep following you.

Do we find people or have people to pull us through our problems. How do we know it's a problem for sure. What do you do when your faced with problems. Knowing and understanding that it's apart of life to constantly go through something. Most of the times it's hard to understand.

Does going through things mean you have to stop living life or enjoying yourself. Maybe we shouldn't focus so much on what's happening instead focus on what's in front of us. When people ask me what's wrong I only talk about how it could be better. I feel that we should make ourselves feel good even in our situations. But how do you focus when is it's around you in you have nowhere to run.

What if we can't really focus what if it's hard to communicate what if there's no one there to listen. How could this be when there's a lot of people out here willing to listen . How can a situation ever change if we don't talk about or try to fix what's going on. If we be scared of our situations then we're scared to change. Who can help us if we're not looking for any help at all.

Who do we believe to trust with our problems. Are there people out here going through the same thing your going through. Do you feel like there's some one or something you can lean on. If there's no feeling of that how can you change it. Finding better and praying would make it easier to want to change.

CHAPTER 5

❧

Family Things

Do you need family or will you always need them. What is the support you get or where does it come from. Why over and over you end up having to feel like your begging from support. Who are these people what happens to people in life. Why do family feel like everything in your life have something to do with them.

What if where we were right now in life was only up to us. We end up with no one to call or help. So what can we do to change that particular situation in our life. How would we fix that without people being there. What makes it hard for people to continue even if no one is there. At first you feel like you need them for everything in your life. In then you find out later some things your going to have to do with out them. Even if it's hard and your steady going through the same things over and over with them. This is setting you up for life to be all on your on. There are a lot of none communicated families.

If their family why don't some have the most faith in you as they should. Why do some not care about where you go in life. How is it every time you get up their bringing you right back down. Who and what do family end up becoming when you really want to make it in life.

What is this thing that holds us from actually getting real support from family. In reality why don't people get support. Why does it mostly come from strangers and friends. What should we really feel coming from family. Maybe we thought we needed family for everything.

Do most hurt come from family why is that. If family is about love in support why does it feel worse than that sometimes. Some of them really shouldn't deserve to be in your life by the things they put you through. Maybe those are the ones you wont need later. Some times you don't even feel nothing coming from them.

The reasons why I found that emptiness else were I had a supporter system. It made me who I am it changed my whole life. When I had no one I counted on my higher support system who used people to help me. I ended up leaving family I was sticking around them. Everything I been through in my life and everything I've been through was only in between the lines of family.

What I've never did was expected people to support me. I know there's a difference between when someone is there for you and there to make sure you need them. Occasionally in life I found out if I don't support myself who else will. People want you to need them but what if we had no one else to need. Then who will we need I've only always counted on and expected god to support me.

Moments before I learned to move on from family. I use to think I needed them for everything. That If they weren't by my side then who will. What if we realize the true only person you need is yourself to start with . Especially later on in life even throughout the things I been through. I was still afraid to lose them or not have them by my side.

Everything I've done in my past my family held that against me like they were prefect themselves. One thing about the things my family brought me through I was able to come out of them. Most of the things I been through I felt like I should blame my family. But I don't I don't blame them because they aren't god. I knew something would get better and that I was never prefect to start with.

This is how you know what's true love you find it out from family. These are people who raise you and protect you and support. We naturally love family right so we automatically know what love is. Love is in family you feel love from family. You just end up knowing the difference between love and hate from family.

At first you feel happiness then you start going through things finally you feel hate. Growing up around my entire family I knew the reason why everyone treated me a certain way. Most of them were hurt them selves or they hated the fact that they couldn't help me. My pain then eventually went away. I've always been glad to be free from people that only hurt me.

The worst people I've ever dealt with. The

closest people to me were people I had to keep fighting off. What was I fighting for. Why did it keep happening who are they if they leave you out. Who are they when they end up needing you.

Do you forgive people do you forget the things you go through. How do we enjoy our family even when they constantly putting you through things. You forget about your problems in love them anyways. For the people they supposed to be or just who they are. Problems eventually go away it's just sometimes hard to get over them.

CHAPTER 6

❧

God

Was I ever enough who made me this way. Why did I have to keep feeling these things. What was I suppose to do. Was something going to ever change were people going to forever feel this way. Who is going to get me out of this forever.

What keeps protecting me from things that I know could be worse. What keeps calling me out of this. What's leading me to a place I thought I'd never find. How do I keep finding out what to do about this. But if god is God why did I keep going through this.

I got saved by god because he chose me. Why did he choose me what was I going to do. God kept me the entire time because he had plans for me. So why be sad about the things your going through forever. When you know god is just going to pull you right out.

But who is Jesus that saves if god does that to. Jesus died on the cross to save us for the sins which he knew we were going to commit. God sends Jesus to do these thing's because God is who chose Jesus who was chosen to save. Who most of us people forget about now. We remember god but not Jesus who sacrificed his life for people who don't even look to him today. I never forgot about who died for me people now remember who won't do a thing for them in reality.

Why does sin keep happening over and over if Jesus died for ours. How do you pray what do you say. Do people even believe that sins are forgiven or do they think that God hold them against us forever. People who really don't know god thinks he hold us accountable for everything we do. When you confess your sins and ask the Lord for forgiveness your automatically healed.

The reason why Jesus died for our sins is because he knows we aren't prefect sins leads you either in two places. The reason we need forgiveness of our sins is to keep us from these two places. Dead or in jail god knows it will and can get worse. When Jesus was risen from the dead he came to save people from their sins he came to lead the people to everlasting life. God knows people are destroying what he has created god uses his son to save his people and his world again.

So why do people put themselves before god. Why do they think their isn't know god. How should they live on a world who was created by power. Do they deserve to be here how does that make god feel. So who was Jesus that came back in the placement of God.

God has rule even over all evil. There was eventually going to be just a matter of time before the world was getting destroyed and Jesus came back with the power. God didn't expect for all his people to believe in him or his son your still his children. He still knows you even the people who think their god. God knows what going on in the world he sees what everyone is doing he knows when he's going to send Jesus.

Does this mean he expected you to turn to him before he knew you didn't believe in him. So what is it when you don't even know how to stop sinning. Does this mean your prefect.

You ask for forgiveness then you do it again. God know you aren't prefect he knows what you should do to not do it again.

This why you need god he can keep you from the things you think are hard to do. Was I prefect did I stop doings things. I wasn't prefect one bit but god made me prefect in his ways. So everything I do from him is just like him. So how do god keep helping you if you keep doing it.

God wants me god loves me just like he does everyone. He had a plan for me he wanted to save me. So everything he knew I was going to do he brought me right from it even though I'm Christian doesn't mean I was always a prefect one. When I got better with god I got better and better. I knew his word more and what it says I knew his plans regarding my life I new who he was more I loved and cherished him more.

Did people understand that or did they have to . No some people didn't like it or didn't understand why I had so much faith. Well I was chosen by god I didn't know how they would understand. Especially if they don't take time to understand him. Did I care no god was obviously more important to me.

When did I realize I was saved or chosen by god. How did I know that I was chosen. When did I get saved. Did I have to get saved or I wanted to be saved. As a baby I was chosen god knew what he had for me he knew what he and some people would take me through. He was going to just bring me right out.

I got saved because one day I didn't believe that was so. He saved me from everything to keep me because what he knew he had for me. So what's in store for non believers is death. What do you mean death are you going to die. Some people will and some people will get saved and some people life will perish forever.

When Jesus comes back you will have no choice but to confess that he is Jesus Christ. When you're a believer non believers don't understand why we still trust god. It's because we know the life of death. Believers know what that leads to. We also know where the true power is.

What do you do when your searching for him but can't get right with him. Do he always here you do he always answer. Why do you go through so much. Why do most believers almost lose their life's following god. Its god we trust things we have to face being a believer it's part of his plan for us to first listen.

Do god sometimes take forever. It isn't that he takes forever he knows just when you need it. He knows your life in what's going on in it. So he won't allow some things to come around in during some situations. Everybody don't need what you need or don't deserve it. Many people say it's luck it's faith and obeying people mess it up for themselves it isn't god fault what people do in their life god only can keep you from it and give you life.

So why don't god save us all from sin if we're all his children. You have to ask him for forgiveness and confess your sins to him. What's sins the opposite of what's right. What's the opposite of what's right the wrong things. So do god still love us even non believers.

God loves everyone that's why he sent his son to save you from what's keeping you whole. Its something you need not from people something feels like your destroyed. Something feels like your know it isn't the same you know you want more. But what is it why I'm still not happy why I'm still doing wrong why I'm still not in my right mind. Its what you've been in so long it's meant to kill and destroy.

Why don't people want to wait on god anyhow. If god didn't create the devil will you just be living with no leader. If he didn't send him back on earth will you just be sinning to be sinning. If he didn't release him to allow him to do things will you just be there sitting on earth. Who would you follow who would you hate will it be Christ Jesus.

So why haven't we yet or eventually will realize who it is God and Jesus Christ is. Why don't we care about him. Why don't we search him why don't we look for him. If he has power over everything you want changed in your life why haven't you found out who Jesus is. Where do you believe power comes what keeps you from good things that last forever. What's the difference between glory and being popular.

Do people hate Jesus and the people that searches him because who he is or what he do. How and when did people know not to search for Jesus. What made people want to be against Jesus do people believe in everlasting life. Do they not believe Jesus will make that happen. Who do people think Jesus is.

Who is he to be a man that lies or leave or for sake you. Who is he to want to kill you or ruin your life. Who is he that will bring you out of everything just to give you all the good things after wards. Who is he that will keep you in every situation and circumstance. Who is he that will lead you astray that gives you patience love and kindness for the everlasting life.

Before I found the true meaning of Jesus I wasn't lost I was still found I just wasn't prefect. I knew what I thought I wanted in life but always knew I would fail many times cause god wanted to keep me anyhow. I thought it was impossible to still choose sin and be saved. To still want to do bad but still there be a bigger picture. Everything in my life has worked out for the better.

Being choose doesn't mean you pick god it means god picks you and wants to use you. I've done many things in my life knowing this. Seen many places knowing this and holding back and on to things knowing this. I didn't know what I truly had until I got closer with Jesus. So why did I wait so long and why did I keep dealing with things.

There was a god he was above all things and kept strengthen me. My worse enemy was myself. I needed to believe that I had a god and a purpose. I wanted to hold on to that. People didn't understand that. Everlasting life was more important then people I knew who would end up leaving in the first place.

They had no rights or didn't belong. I was temporarily in a spot to be able to hold on what god promised. People kept wanting to take that but they couldn't. They were ruining their life cause god was above that not me. Its like trying to take from god people didn't understand the rights of God.

I kept following god even though I was losing myself sometimes even people. Sometimes being a believer you actually go through the worst of pains. You wouldn't expect the types of people that will turn on you. Especially from ones you thought you would need after all in the long run. Who is it that only end up needing and who kept keeping me is who I ended up with forever.

God was my true miracle and blessing for my life. I couldn't go through some of the things I went through alone. Sometimes I would think is life worth living. God kept me from all that. It was a long journey.

CHAPTER 7

❧

Escape

Plans are ideas we have for ourselves and our futures. What do we try to get away from. When do we know when to create these plans. When do we know we need them. Will they work how far will they take us.

Do you need people to help you in certain areas of your plan yes. Will there be people there to help you yes. I started running off very early. I wanted to be different so I would always choose different things.

But was I ever distracted by things that would sometimes make it hard for me. I didn't understand what I wanted once upon a time I just new I wanted to be different. What seemed so different to me. What did I want to do why did I keep on trying to get away. Did I know what I was trying to get away from.

How do you come up with a plan for your life if you don't know what you want. How do you know what you want. When do you know you want that. Does it take certain steps that you have to follow. What is it we know we need but won't go get.

How long did it take me. What was keeping me away. Was it pain was it demons was it my situations. Really it's easy to figure out what you need to get away from. If something doesn't ever go away you know it's more deeper than a story to tell. Some people life changes because of how deep things are in their life.

I kept on going through the same things over and over. I didn't know when I was coming out of them or how. But I knew one thing I was surly getting away from everything. Even if I had know meaning of getting away I wanted to consider anyway. Did anyone ever try to stop me.

Somethings hurt so bad I felt like the only choice was to leave. Did things ever try to follow me yes. I never felt welcomed I never felt comfort by things that pushing me away. My life was really hard because of what I wanted. People have up on me for things I didn't know or wanted.

But why do these things always have to be the cause we have to stop trying. It never was right to be in the same situation over and over. But how about going through the same thing over and over but with different people. I kept running then I once stopped running. I knew I would eventually get over it.

Why did I run If I had plans. Was it easy just to follow through with them and ignore everything else. Sometimes getting away was apart of my plan. Somethings I do today I never would have last year. Mostly I can't believe leaving was the best thing that happened to me

It took me a while to take one step. I was deep in fear I was totally distracted. By what everything I wasn't fully or potentially ready for anything. I lost everything I had. I was doing a lot of bad things getting into a lot of bad situations. I was pregnant with nothing at all.

What I started to do was believe in my self more in more. Keep trusting God and keep working on my plans and praying. I knew if

I kept doing this I would find myself right were god wants me to be. Why did I loose everything and not just get it. It was really hard for me but this is what made me .

So how do you do things with nothing how do it work. Why you just can't find another way. Was it hard to do the normal thing anybody else would do. Well my life was different I had people to support me but I had no one to actually be there in help me. I eventually felt like people were unable to help me in this.

Well what do you do when you have a plan and you have nothing. You trust you plan you take action and someone will help you regardless. I used to tell people about my plans so they know if I needed help what area would they be able to support.

But I was wrong no one could help me at all with my plans. I kept sharing them and trying to include people and pull people in it. I found out it was different for me. I never stopped trying or believing in what I wanted. It was only right to keep getting away from people who wasn't apart of my plan.

I did love my life and everyone in it. Sometimes you just don't always want to live the same or be the same as everyone. Most of the time we can't help who we are. Definitely who we were made to be. I kept bettering my self the further I got. I had a lot of hard times and things that may held me back but I kept getting through everything.

The reason I found my self getting away because every time I would lean on some-one that wasn't the person I needed. Anyone could be there but I doesn't have to be who you need. My life literally was my educator my life taught me things and grew me from things. I surly did need that because what's plan or being better with things and people you don't need.

CHAPTER 8

❦

Death

This is what tried to keep me from life. Before I lived I almost died plenty of times. I could've been gone along time ago but when I found life something happened to me. Better yet when life found me.

Death isn't just something that happens to us physically.

Usually I would think that wasn't so important. You would think everyone will die some day. That's true but that isn't how it happens. Your obligated to live a long prosperous life with out anything happening to you that will kill you but could but won't. Sometimes people get life and death mixed up they don't know how it works.

Spiritually you are protected therefore you

may not know what's going but because of what you believe. You are going to be kept enough to get you out of it or keep you from it. My times of trouble were wild and crazy. The reason I went through because I had to experience death first. So what's death if we're still here what's death if you almost died believing as well.

Not a prosperous life so you could start out but it's were you end up later. Well why people that aren't of death aren't prosperous at first. To believe in the life you already have or finally own it. You have to go through the one that will keep you from it first

I learned how to live a prosperous life before I finally got it. I didn't understand what's living of death if everyone still living happy or sad. The important thing about it was what I chose to settle for in my life. Did I want to understand what life was. Was there a bigger to life did I even care were life took me I just thought it was about living.

Actually I found out about it because the life I was searching for I really didn't have to search for. I was going through things it didn't keep me from life though. It kept be here to understand the difference between life and death. People don't really understand how important life actually is and what you chose until it's too late.

What is it that some people are of death but rich and famous. Why are they enjoying life their living it up. Was or is it really a difference long as your happy. People could do whatever but it's actually more important than you think. Death destroys people and it almost destroyed me.

I wouldn't judge people of death only god could but I can help led you how I was led. Sometimes I used to think it would be easy getting here. Not knowing my life was just as hard as anyone's dealing with life and death.

You wonder do people live just to die. I didn't think I had to worry about that until I start finding life. Just as soon as it found me. Everyone has someone or something they want to living for but are you living just to die. What does that mean I'm still here death is what happens physically but what end up happening to you in your life.

I've really went to death and back to life. Fighting off death because I wanted life was hard. You gain and you loose a lot of people. The good thing that always have came out of that was I still amounted to the things life was trying to give me. Nothing comes hard when believing or not regardless of your state what are you doing with it.

Some people say it never really occurred to me or mattered. I'm sharing what I know and what it took me to actually live. It was the things I didn't know and of the things I did know. I remember some of the worst things I could ever imagine is actually seeing the dead when their in people then they cross over leaves the other to perish. How do I know that you don't have control over your self.

You only could have control over your mind. And your own behaviors depending on what kind of choice your making. what wants to destroy is either in you or always with you. The spiritual thing about it is I found out really everyone has a gift. People destroy it because they don't try to find the person who gave it to them. So instead they choose death so they take it and death is what messes up your lives.

CHAPTER 9

❧

Love

God grew not only from the inside but also the out. I knew I felt love when every situation and every trail came with something new. Being guided and protected in and out of my situation. The greatest love of all something that never goes away. What happens if we don't know what love feels like or what it means.

I started experiencing gods love early in my life Yet at first I thought it was just me. Even when I wasn't close to him I felt his love around me over me and trying to get through me. It's the prefect feeling you get when you know there's no other feeling like it.

No one could take gods love away from me.

People have tried numerous of times. So if someone tells you that you don't know what love is they don't know god. God is love in his love is through us and in us. How can you be too young to know what love is if you believe in god he is love and everything about him is love.

Sometimes people find their self searching for the wrong things in life. When you want to find true love try to find it in god. God is love therefore if we really don't know his love how can we ever find true love. What do you expect from god about love. What are the things you want god to help you with.

I didn't try to find love my problems were always loving too fast and forgiving too easy. Right when I feel lonely I do these things .We aren't prefect but only in gods way of making us prefect. When I got use to being with god I knew that was all I needed first.

Normally this wouldn't be the topic. But I rather say I know a lot of people out here are searching for people. Most of us don't won't to be alone or are afraid to be alone. Why is that we feel like living someone physically is more important than loving ourselves first. Why is it that were afraid to be alone or don't won't to be alone.

Do you feel like you can't make it or just the thought of flesh need of someone or something there. How can you possibly feel like you need something or someone first before yourself. How can you pull it together if your mentally damaged and want to continue to need someone. Before giving yourself time to heal from the last thing or person that was in your life.

Damaged from love also what does that mentally or emotionally mean does this feeling change. Well we can't see what one goes through but we sure can move on and love ourselves eventually. Time heals Everything so what does this mean. God is love I do believe people should find love in god. What does this mean once you get to know god you'll know his love.

I truly didn't know what this meant from a person but I sure did believe in god and I fell deeply in love with god. So there wasn't know other feeling I've felt before than the love from god. Gods love is powerful it's strong it's unconditional it's priceless. You couldn't find it nowhere else if you didn't have the love of God first. My whole entire point was understanding what's the love of god.

Truly I've opened up to god about everything. He has saved me from people and places I would never go back to. I found my self numerous of times falling to fast and forgiving to easy. Knowing it was absolutely dangerous for me personally and mentally.

Starting to fall in love with god was all I wanted to do and feel. He brought me out and he has brought me in. No other feeling but the feeling from god could change my love I have for god. It is true love receiving and worshipping god. He teaches and takes you through things that's Boone would be able to take you out of.

When I go over love I go over the love of God. Especially how I received it and how it makes me feel. Well if I'm In love right now what's that feeling I feel. Not going over no one else's love life but explaining what's god love life is. What it's like to love god how does it makes us feel.

Sometimes I use to wonder is anyone ever going to love me. How will I love myself if I'm waiting to be loved. I then realized I've always been loved by god. How did I know what's the feeling I felt when I did find my

self in love with god. To me god only mattered I was prefect being in love with god but
I sure was able to do everything he I could do.

What is the love of god. It's Spiritual love
it's not being able to turn from god. You get
closer you feel safer you feel protected wher-
ever you go. There's no one that will keep you
from it. I didn't start off being so in love with
god I ended up being deeply in love .

He changed everything about my life.
Things that I were going through being young
and lost or being traumatized. Being tired of
loving people to fast catching feeling too fast.
Loving too easy I learned the love of God
being young that's all I needed. I knew one
day eventually god will heal that spot once he
knows I was ready.

I was very young getting into many relation-
ships but that's what young people do. Actually I wasn't prefect until I found the prefect
ness in god. This is what makes us prefect.
Prefect in all my ways in all my situations and
circumstances. The earlier I start learning god
the more I start making my own decisions.

The later and closer I got in god the deeper
god has showed me that I won't find nothing
out here if it's not of him. I say love because

this is what we all search for. But not me I've always had ships and felt fast

I wouldn't say happier alone but I'm better knowing god knows what's best for me. He gives me everything I need in the end and take away what I don't need. Knowing that one day he will eventually show up with that. So I learned that fact that I'm s deep in god that and being so young with all my mistakes. Not to search love this soon it finds you sooner later.

This soon is the growing stage of a person. So being young I wasn't finding love I was growing. So what is it when we can't stop dealing with some one or something. What happens when we're attached to someone or something. What happens if they showing us a feeling we've never felt.

Knowing the love of God I know that true love is in god. People can't give you what god can. We are physically mentally and emotionally growing from these people and these things. These are the stages we need to grow in these are feelings we are feeling because we're afraid. Eventually we will be happy but I know everything that is loved or will be loved in my life is the love of God.

If it comes from god it is true love. Everything I've been through grew me out of something I needed to grow from. How can I be so young looking and finding love. When first I needed to love god. People really don't know love until they know god. Some situations people are in is because of things they are growing from and need to grow on.

So what did I learn about love that it isn't true if it doesn't have god. So what is it People do. I have no idea but I know if it isn't god it isn't true. God is true everything he gives and everything he takes away. If it hurt it's something that needs to grow or needs to heal. Everything won't be prefect.

I've just learned so much about god and finding god. Its basically things god have taught me. By showing me telling and me reading it. Basically I've spent my whole god life's journey searching and following god. So my experiences with god and following god has been particular based upon wisdom and truth.

I've out grown the things that aren't from god. Also I've over thrown the things which tries to take gods place. I know being young it sounds crazy but god didn't think so. Nothing

was too hard for him using anyone or anything he is true. God knew what he wanted
to do in my life. He knew where he wanted to
take me he knew the things I was going to go
through. But there isn't no other way to say I
have loved god as long as I followed him.

Its sounds wired to some people but I put
god before everything in my life. People
have never understood that. I'm young and it
wasn't easy at first but I chose to always listen
and obey god. It was the truth and the love I
had from him and for him. If you knew god
you would not feel like you can't get out of
things or that nothing would never work. The
fact that god loves and protects and provides
he also keeps.

Purposely drawn to the love of Jesus Christ.
I knew god had loved me more than I loved
myself. There was know doubt in the world
that it was going to be any different. It was
easy to imagine what my life would be like
with god in it. How did I know I was drawn
by gods love.

No other person in the world seemed to
be more important to me than god. Sometimes people don't understand that feeling of
gods love because he draws you to him by his

Spirit. I felt his love inside and out I felt it in my heart that I knew there was always someone there. It couldn't get took away from me it was true. What if there wasn't a god how would we know love.

If people love how do they know it's true without knowing what loving god is. How does love feel real if you haven't yet felt the love of god. If you never experienced what god love is how do you know it's real. Why do I talk about love this is the love of god. God is love and love is in god.

Many times in my life I have never felt such a strong connection. God is mainly my main person I count on in my life. I've always looked to god with everything and every situation. He never turned his back on me. When so many people did I had someone left that was there and it wasn't a lover it was more like my friend.

When things gotten ugly I had a brighter day. Most of the times I will feel empty and lost. Sometimes people would allow this feeling to occur. So much often god would protect guide heal and cover those who love him and those he loves. The reason I'm so into god is because I feel like god is the only love in my life that would understand me better than the people who was supposed to love me which is family.

be more important to me than god. Sometimes people don't understand that feeling of gods love because he draws you to him by his Spirit. I felt his love inside and out I felt it in my heart that I knew there was always someone there. It couldn't get took away from me it was true. What if there wasn't a god how would we know love.

If people love how do they know it's true without knowing what loving god is. How does love feel real if you haven't yet felt the love of god. If you never experienced what god love is how do you know it's real. Why do I talk about love this is the love of god. God is love and love is in god.

Many times in my life I have never felt such a strong connection. God is mainly my main person I count on in my life. I've always looked to god with everything and every situation. He never turned his back on me. When so many people did I had someone left that was there and it wasn't a lover it was more like my friend.

When things gotten ugly I had a brighter

day. Most of the times I will feel empty and lost. Sometimes people would allow this feeling to occur. So much often god would protect guide heal and cover those who love him and those he loves. The reason I'm so into god is because I feel like god is the only love in my life that would understand me better than the people who was supposed to love me which is family.

CHAPTER 10

❧

The Spirit

Purposely walking in my promise was something I had endured from god. What it's like to be full of the spirit. What it's like to walk in the spirit. The spirit is live it's meaningful and anointing. How did I know I was in the spirit was because of I could feel when it was around and I knew that it was in me.

The things I were going through were healed and covered by the spirit. So what is the spirit it's gods presence. Its who God is his surrounding his shadow. The most exciting thing about this is there wasn't know other spirit like it.

How did I know whenever the spirit was around. Did I know what the difference was in the presence. I had to learn this as well I had to understand this u had to get wisdom and truth on this. My battles for god hadn't being easy learning and worshipping. I've figured out who battles they were or sometimes why I was constantly in them.

Did I just believe in the spirit did the spirit help me. What does it mean to be led by the spirit. Well of course we can't see god physically one day he although could make that appearance. Likely people of god are lead. By the spirit of God in things they do and things they receive.

Not every situation in our life is god some of it is our flesh or us. Why do some people say if god Is god why does this keep happening or why god. My conclusion is you didn't here god say it ne didn't do it. How do you here god say it even through his spirit. Preachers people his word places and sometimes things.

Being led by the spirit. God will speak directly to your situation and you will feel it. When I first felt the spirit I was crying very strong. I was lying down in the bed on my phone. Searching on you tube as always I had gotten into a bad car wreck a couple days before this.

Listening to that woman speak to me on

you tube. I clicked on a video to start viewing I was already scrolling so I clicked on it. She started preaching in then she started speaking to what I just went through telling me what had happened. This was the moment I knew the spirit was trying to come to me in a better way and I needed the spirit more.

I had the spirit already but since god wanted me for something I was his chosen one. He wanted to keep me connected to his spirit so that I could hear him. God was already in my life I just needed to follow him. He was protecting me already through everything I was going through god was trying to make me Prefect. He knew I was going to make decisions being young and do things he wouldn't do but I had to learn more about him. God chose me and lifted me up higher by his spirit because God is a spirit that we feel hear and love. I didn't know my life had changed this early.

A spirit I've never gave up on a spirit who has never left my side in any situation. Everything about my life is about the spirit now. I know what I have been able to overcome and the reason the spirit has brought me out of it. There was no other place I had rather been spiritually than with the spirit of God. Who rain forever so how do you get led by the spirit. God led me because I needed to get closer with him. I seeked him more and stay connected to him more I learned his truth I understood that you could do anything and come out of anything with him. No matter how hard it gets or how long it takes that battle is not yours it's gods because God uses his power every time. Some people don't understand how powerful and mighty God is. They don't really acknowledge the fact that god is god and he is powerful and mighty above everything and everybody . So I kept believing it myself the more I believed the more he showed his power. So who would god be not to protect and heal and bless. Who is it that does those things who brings us out of situations we can't come out of on our own. Imagine being in some thing you didn't understand or can't get out of.

ABOUT THE AUTHOR

KEARA COMBS is a very wise god strengthen young lady. Who was born in Little Rock. But grew up also in North Little Rock. She has been through a lot in her life being only 23 years old she found god at an early age. She had been discovering god all of her developed stages of her life. Not only does she like touching other people's souls but also she likes for people to learn more about god. She has a lot in store in her life. Gaining full access of the unknown. While losing a lot she wants to touch other people who are lost. Being very Loving and dedicated to the world she wants to share god. This was her first book she wrote may not be the last she hopes that people just feel it not having to understand she just want to show people what's been true in her life hoping it becomes a truth in yours.

J. Kenkade
PUBLISHING®

Writing Workshops
We'll help you write it.

Virtual Sessions

For help with writing your story:
www.jkenkadepublishing.com
(501) 482-JKEN

Also Available from J. Kenkade Publishing

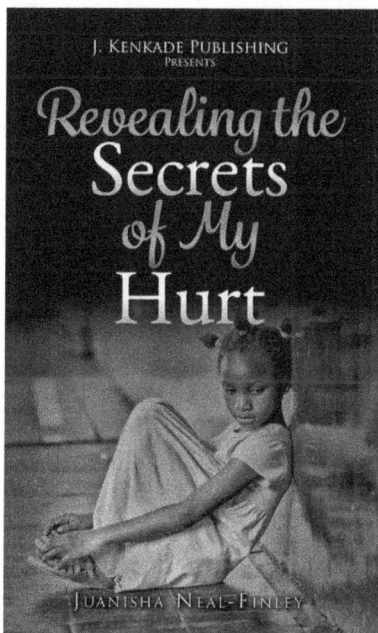

ISBN: 978-1-944486-13-6
Purchase at www.amazon.com

Captivating. Step into the life story of a young girl tormented by an abusive family. Young Cindy rewrites her experiences with a mother introduced to drugs, sexual abuse from her father, and death. Cindy reveals how strong God can make anyone in the midst of Satan's schemes. Experience her journey in "Revealing the Secrets of My Hurt."

Also Available from
J. Kenkade Publishing

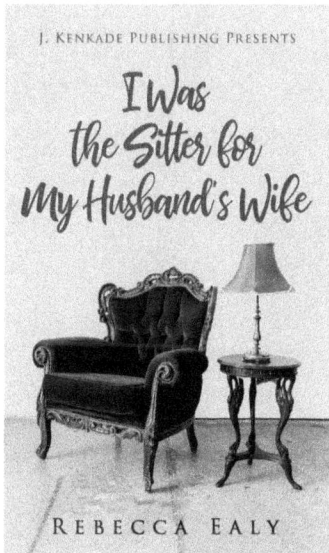

J. KENKADE PUBLISHING PRESENTS

I Was
the Sitter for
My Husband's Wife

REBECCA EALY

An engaging story about a single woman living far away from her family. Rebekah finds herself needing more fulfillment in her life as a nurse. She has been praying to God for her need until one day, He finally answers in the form of two strangers who aren't really strangers at all.

Available for purchase at www.amazon.com
Paperback 978-1-944486-17-4

Also Available from
J. Kenkade Publishing

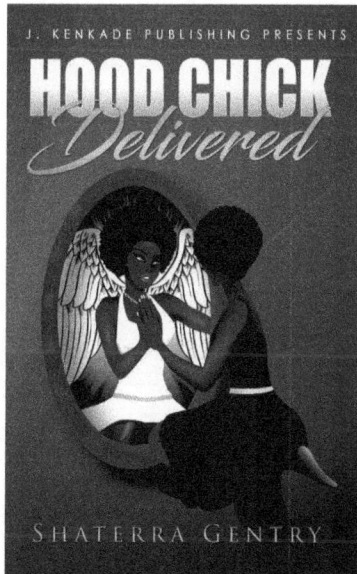

Hood Chick delivered describes a woman's troubled past as she is introduced to stripping and violence. After a friend gets shot and put into a coma for a few months, Layna cries out unto God, who tells her to commit to a life of Christ so that her friend may be saved. This novel describes a life that falls into submission with God, after a life of defiance with the devil.

Available for purchase at www.amazon.com
Paperback 978-1-944486-16-7

www.ingramcontent.com/pod-product-compliance
Lightning Source LLC
LaVergne TN
LVHW011215080426
835508LV00007B/804